Pasco County Library System
Overdue notices are a courtesy of the Library System.
Failure to receive an overdue notice does not absolve the borrower of the obligation to return the materials on time.

SCIENCE ON THE EDGE

PREDICTING NATURAL DISASTERS

WRITTEN BY
JOHN ALLEN

BLACKBIRCH PRESS
An imprint of Thomson Gale, a part of The Thomson Corporation

THOMSON
™
GALE

LAND O'LAKES
BRANCH

Detroit • New York • San Francisco • San Diego • New Haven, Conn. • Waterville, Maine • London • Munich

Photo credits: U.S. Geological Survey, cover; AFP/Getty Images, 26, 45; AP/Wide World Photos, 12, 16, 20, 24, 25, 30, 38, 42; © Bettmann/CORBIS, 9; © Bob Krist/CORBIS, 7; EPA/Landov, 29; Ethan Miller/Reuters/Landov, 40; Franck Robichon/EPA/Landov, 21; Jean-Loup Charmet/Photo Researchers, Inc., 10; Joe Skipper/Reuters/Landov, 5; KCNA/EPA/Landov, 36; Kyodo/Landov, 39; Mauro Fermariello/Photo Researchers, Inc., 11; NASA Jet Propulsion Laboratory, 35; NASA/JPL/NIMA, 22; NASA/JPL/QuikSAT Science Team, 44; National Oceanic & Atmospheric Administration, 15, 18; National Weather Service/EPA/Landov, 31; Photos.com, 14, 37, 41; U.S. Geological Survey, 13; U.S. Geological Survey/Cascades Volcano Observatory, 33; Wolfgang Rattay/Reuters/Landov, 4

LIBRARY OF CONGRESS CATALOGING-IN-PUBLICATION DATA

Allen, John, 1957–
    Predicting natural disasters / by John Allen.
        p. cm. — (Science on the edge)
    Includes bibliographical references and index.
    ISBN 1-4103-0717-4 (hard cover : alk. paper)
    1. Natural disaster warning systems—Juvenile literature. 2. Natural disasters—Juvenile literature. I. Title. II. Series.

    GB5030.A45 2005
    363.34'72—dc22   2005013253

Printed in the United States of America
10 9 8 7 6 5 4 3 2 1

TABLE OF CONTENTS

Introduction: *The Toll of Natural Disasters* 4

Chapter One: *The History of Predicting Natural Disasters* 6

Chapter Two: *Predicting Natural Disasters Today* 20

Chapter Three: *The Future of Predicting Natural Disasters* . . .33

Glossary 46

For Further Information 47

Index 47

About the Author 48

THE TOLL OF NATURAL DISASTERS

Each year, natural disasters cause tens of thousands of deaths worldwide. Some of these events, such as earthquakes, volcanic eruptions, and tsunamis, are the result of shifting plates beneath the earth's crust. Others, such as hurricanes, tornadoes, and flood-producing rains, originate in the atmosphere around the planet. Often, these disasters seem to strike without warning. Aside from the toll they take on human life, they can also disrupt food production, destroy homes, and wipe out wildlife, farms, and factories.

In general, less-developed countries are the hardest hit when a disaster strikes. For example, a 2003 earthquake in Bam, Iran, an ancient city filled with fragile structures, killed 26,000 people. The

A rescue worker and his specially trained dog search for signs of survivors after a powerful earthquake leveled the Iranian city of Bam in 2003.

A highway and many homes and businesses in Gulf Shores, Alabama, lie submerged beneath several feet of water after Hurricane Ivan in 2004.

cost of caring for the injured, importing food and clean water, restoring electrical power and other utilities, and repairing damaged streets and buildings had to be shared with wealthier nations. A single disaster can cripple an impoverished area for years.

To limit the destructive potential of natural disasters, scientists are working on new technologies to predict where and when they are most likely to strike. Their tools range from computer networks to weather satellites to machines that measure the slightest vibrations of the earth. Science may never be able to predict the exact moment an earthquake will strike or the precise path a hurricane will take. However, new technologies are helping to manage the risks from nature's most dangerous events.

CHAPTER 1

THE HISTORY OF PREDICTING NATURAL DISASTERS

Ancient people had many different explanations for earthquakes and volcanoes. In India, Hindu myths described a flat earth balanced on the backs of eight gigantic elephants. When one grew weary and bowed its back, an earthquake would shake the ground. Peruvian stories blamed earthquakes on the thunderous footsteps of a god coming down to earth. The ancient Greek philosopher Aristotle thought that earthquakes and volcanic eruptions resulted from hot winds moving inside the planet.

Earthquakes are actually caused by the movement of giant slabs inside the earth called tectonic plates. These plates float atop the earth's mantle, a thick layer of rock and molten material that surrounds the hot core of the planet. The plates travel past each other at different speeds, and sometimes one plate forces itself beneath another. The resulting pressure builds up until the rocks of the stressed crust above suddenly break apart. An earthquake begins at the focus point where the rocks break, spreading shock waves in every direction.

EARLY STUDIES OF EARTHQUAKES

Throughout history, people have studied the phenomenon of earthquakes in resourceful ways. In A.D. 132, a Chinese scholar named Chang Heng built the dragon jar, the first instrument used to record data about an earthquake. The device featured a series of metal dragons, each with a ball in its mouth, arranged around a jar and connected to a lever inside it. When the ground shook in an earthquake and the jar was stirred, the dragons would release the balls into the mouths of metal frogs around the foot of the jar. The ingenious device could show the first trembling impulse of an earthquake.

Records of earthquakes go back 3,000 years, to the beginning of a Chinese catalog that recorded every moderate to large quake in China, and have been maintained up to the present day. The first systematic study of earthquakes began in 1755, after one of history's most deadly earthquakes struck Lisbon, Portugal. More than 100,000

This deep rift valley in Iceland formed when two tectonic plates pulled apart.

THE CONTINENTAL DRIFT THEORY

In the twentieth century, scientists realized that earthquakes and volcanoes were the result of plate tectonics. The crust beneath the earth's surface is made up of a series of plates. Convection currents, or currents of heat rising from the planet's core, move the crustal plates in different directions.

Plate tectonics also asserts that the continents themselves are moving. A look at a globe of the earth shows that the continents seem to fit together like puzzle pieces. For example, the east coast of South America makes a snug fit with the west coast of Africa. Were these huge landmasses once connected?

In 1912, a German scientist named Alfred Wegener proposed that all the continents were once joined in one huge supercontinent he named Pangaea. Through a process called continental drift that had occurred over millions of years, they had gradually broken apart and drifted into their present configuration. Wegener explained mountain ranges as colossal folds that occurred when two plates collided. He also noted that fossils of identical plants and animals had been found across the Atlantic Ocean from each other. Scientists had explained this fact by postulating that land bridges, now sunk beneath the seas, had once connected the continents. Professional geologists scorned Wegener as an amateur in the field, and they ridiculed his theory.

Nevertheless, later research confirmed Wegener's ideas. In the 1950s, scientists discovered ridges at the bottom of the ocean as large as mountain ranges. These ridges were the result of seafloor spreading, with molten material rising up from the joints between crustal plates. Scientists came to realize that the huge plates were indeed moving and shifting—just as Wegener had described. Wegener died in 1930 without knowing that his ideas would one day become accepted science.

In 1912, German scientist Alfred Wegener (above) theorized that all of the earth's continents were once joined together in a landmass he called Pangaea (below).

This eighteenth-century illustration shows the people of Lisbon fleeing in terror as buildings collapse during an earthquake in 1755.

people died from the quake and the related tsunami. A tsunami is a huge wave created when an earthquake rocks the ocean floor. In Lisbon, the quake first ripped fissures through the downtown streets. Then citizens watched from the docks in amazement as ocean waters receded to reveal the bare seafloor littered with old shipwrecks. A few seconds later, the sea returned as a gigantic wall of water that engulfed the harbor and much of the city.

Sebastião de Melo, Portugal's prime minister, set out to study the occurrence in detail. He sent a list of detailed questions to every priest in the region. He asked how long the earthquake had lasted, how many aftershocks were felt, and whether animals in the area had behaved strangely in any way. The responses were archived, and have been studied in detail by contemporary scientists. For his resourcefulness in gathering information, de Melo is considered one of the founders of seismology (from the Greek *seismos* or "shock"), which is the study of earthquakes.

In 1855, an Italian named Luigi Palmieri invented the seismoscope, a device used to record the time and motion of an earthquake. Palmieri's instrument had a conical weight suspended over a basin of mercury on a spiral spring. A slight vertical motion, such as an earthquake, caused the tip of the cone to make contact

In 1855, Luigi Palmieri invented the seismoscope, which recorded the time an earthquake occurred and its motion.

THE RICHTER SCALE

In order for scientists to share information about earthquakes, they needed a measuring scale to use as a basis for comparing quakes in different areas. In 1935, an American named Charles Richter invented just such a mathematical scale for measuring the intensity of earthquakes. The Richter scale expresses the

In 1935, Charles Richter devised a mathematical scale to quantify the intensity of earthquakes.

magnitude of an earthquake as a number from 1 to 7+. Most news reports about earthquakes describe the intensity of the event by referring to its measurement on the Richter scale. For example, the major earthquake in Bam, Iran, measured 6.5 on the Richter scale, while the 2004 earthquake that produced tsunami waves in South Asia has been estimated at over 9.0—making it one of the largest quakes in history.

with the mercury, which completed an electrical circuit and stopped a clock, showing the exact time of the quake. Palmieri's seismoscope also could detect and record horizontal motion. The closing of the electrical circuit set a roll of paper into motion and pressed the tip of a pencil against the paper's surface. Thus, the duration and magnitude of the quake were recorded by the curving pencil mark on paper.

ADVANCES IN SEISMOLOGY AND A NETWORK OF RECORDING STATIONS

In the 1890s, a group of British scientists in Japan, where quakes are frequent, improved on Palmieri's invention. Geologist John

In this aerial photo, California's San Andreas Fault appears as a large fracture in the earth's crust.

Eighteenth-century English meteorologist Luke Howard created a categorization scheme for clouds, such as these cumulus clouds, to help predict weather patterns.

Milne led a group who developed a more accurate seismograph that could record the intensity and duration of an earthquake. The new device featured a pendulum arm that registered the shocks as oscillations, or waves, on a metal disc (and, later, on paper).

With funding from the Royal Society, a prestigious scientific group in England, Milne also set up a series of seismic recording stations. Milne's network eventually linked 40 stations, including sites in Great Britain, Russia, Canada, the eastern coast of the United States, and even Antarctica. The forerunner of today's World-Wide Standard Seismological Network, Milne's network enabled scientists to study earthquakes systematically and share information about them. It also brought about remote sensing, the practice of measuring earthquakes that occur in one area of the earth from a distant region.

The shared research led to mapping of the plates and fault lines beneath the earth. A fault is a fracture in the earth's crust where the layers of rock have been displaced upward or downward. Scientists soon discovered global patterns in earthquake activity—for example, that earthquakes were most likely to occur along faults. A basis for predicting earthquakes was at hand.

EARLY ATTEMPTS AT WEATHER PREDICTION

Predicting storms can be as important as predicting earthquakes, and just as challenging. The ancient Greeks called the study of weather meteorology, or "the study of meteors." To them, a meteor was anything in the sky between the earth and the moon —including clouds, rainbows, rain, hail, and fog. Greek scientists were successful in describing the water cycle and movements of warm and cold air. Some even made bold predictions of fine weather and rich harvests that delighted the people when they

This map from 1872 was one of the earliest maps used for predicting the weather.

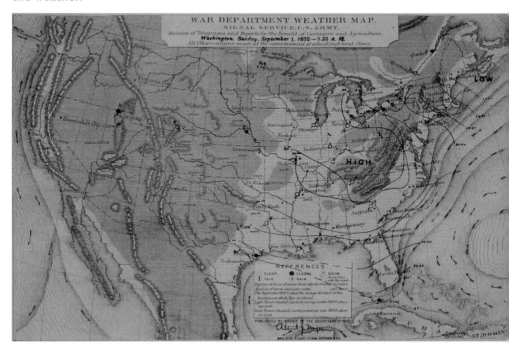

When a cold front and a warm front collide, the collision can sometimes create a tornado.

came true—and, of course, sparked angry responses when they did not.

Weather predicting remained uncertain for centuries, until more systematic work began in the 1700s. England's Luke Howard made breakthroughs in the study of clouds. Howard not only correctly described what a cloud was—warm air that has risen and then cooled to the dew point—but he also categorized clouds by shape, altitude, and how they were formed. He observed that different kinds of clouds offered clues for predicting the weather. For instance, a large mass of cumuli, or low, puffy clouds, in a strong wind meant the approach of calm air and rain.

THE TELEGRAPH AND THE DISCOVERY OF FRONTS

Despite Howard's discoveries, weather prediction was still too haphazard to attract much confidence from ordinary people. What was needed was a way to make reliable long-range weather forecasts for large areas. This required better communication about air masses and their movements. In the 1840s, the invention of the telegraph allowed scientists to instantly share weather observations across great distances. In crude form, meteorologists used the reports to draw weather maps that showed wind patterns and the movement of storm systems.

Still, forecasts were accurate only to about 24 hours. More long-range predictions became possible only with the discovery that masses of air called fronts move in regular patterns. Vilhelm Bjerknes, a Danish meteorologist, noticed that when a cold air mass from the North Pole collided with a warm air mass from the equator, the result was a line that produced storms—like a string of lit firecrackers exploding in sequence.

Fronts react according to basic physics. A cold front moving under a warm front forces the warm air to rise rapidly and spin counterclockwise around a low-pressure center, forming strong thunderstorms with high winds. Sometimes, if the temperature extremes are great enough and other conditions are right, the collision can spawn spout-shaped whirlwinds called tornadoes. Not all collisions of air masses produce storms, however. Should air masses meet without moving, a stationary front is formed. This results in clear or partly cloudy skies. Bjerknes's work allowed meteorologists to track the movement of fronts and forecast weather changes days in advance. He earned a great deal of respect from his entire profession.

WEATHER FORECASTING GOES GLOBAL

In 1939, one of Bjerknes's students made another breakthrough. Carl-Gustaf Rossby discovered great horizontal waves of air that follow the eastward movement of air like ocean waves follow the tides. These Rossby waves, as they came to be called, steer warm and cold air masses through the upper atmosphere. It is as if the

In 1936, meteorologists prepare to launch a weather balloon attached to a radiosonde.

waves are invisible tracks moving on a path at a velocity that can be calculated. Using Rossby's discovery, meteorologists could predict the speed and movement of weather systems around the world with remarkable accuracy.

WEATHER BALLOONS AND COMPUTERS

With the invention of radio and television, weather information passed among scientists faster than ever. Lightweight transmitters called radiosondes were released into the atmosphere tethered to weather balloons and sent back data on temperature, air pressure, and humidity. Most important, in the 1950s, meteorologists began to enlist computers in their efforts to predict the weather. A powerful computer could process ten thousand bits of information from around the globe and use them to produce a detailed forecast for any area. The ability to predict hurricanes and tornadoes, heavy rains, and even droughts with amazing accuracy promised to bring meteorology into the modern age.

CHAPTER 2

PREDICTING NATURAL DISASTERS TODAY

In the decades since the discovery of tectonic plates, scientists have made great advances in understanding what causes earthquakes. Predicting exactly when and where one will occur, however, is still more art than science. Nevertheless, there have been successes in short-term prediction.

In February 1975, the Chinese government ordered three large cities in the Haicheng-Yingkou area to evacuate. The orders were based on a series of observations. One year before, in the same area,

Construction workers attach a rubberized cushioning device under Utah's Capitol building to make it earthquake-safe.

A technician at an emergency response center in Japan monitors data from different types of sensing equipment as he watches for signs of impending disaster.

the ground surface at the Jinzhou fault showed a movement of 0.1 inch (2.5mm) in only nine months. Scientists near Haicheng reported unusual fluctuations in earth's magnetic field. In addition, several amateur observers found changes in the groundwater level including unusual tilts in the ground. Farmers even claimed that livestock were behaving strangely.

Obeying the evacuation order, people slept outdoors in tents despite the winter cold. Two days after the order, an earthquake measuring 7.3 on the Richter scale leveled the cities of Haicheng and Yingkou. The total number of casualties is unknown and occurred mostly on the cities' outskirts, but observers agree that the number would have been far greater if the evacuation had not occurred.

Agencies such as the U.S. Geological Survey forecast earthquakes based on past history and probabilities. These forecasts are called hazard assessments. By comparing data on the location and size of earthquakes in the past, scientists can predict the likelihood of future quakes in an area. The assessments are broken into three time scales: long-term, intermediate, and short-term. Long-term assessments, say experts, are especially helpful because they allow cities to prepare for disasters. For example, a city might toughen building codes to make buildings safer and improve warning systems so people can react quickly when an earthquake is forecast.

NASA'S QUAKESIM PROGRAM

One earthquake prediction program with a remarkable success rate is NASA's QuakeSim. Scientists at QuakeSim use a variety of high-tech tools to forecast earthquakes. Detailed data about past earthquakes are developed into computer models that predict when these events might recur along the same fault lines. Satellites in space make precision measurements of changes in rock formations around high-risk areas. Powerful radar also scans these areas for slight changes due to stress and flow along fault lines. Super-computers process all this data to create earthquake forecasts much like weather forecasts.

QuakeSim has also made a map of California divided into 4,000 boxes, or tiles. Researchers use computer models to find each tile's earthquake potential. The tiles are then color-coded according to

This topographical satellite image of California's San Fernando Valley can help seismologists assess the potential for future quakes in the area.

risk. Beginning around 1995, the program correctly predicted the locations of all but one of California's sixteen largest earthquakes. QuakeSim scientists believe their scorecard approach can be adapted to quake-prone areas around the world.

THE SOUTH ASIA TSUNAMIS AND PROBLEMS WITH EARLY WARNING

Even the best earthquake-predicting techniques make little difference without a way of quickly getting the information to people in the threatened area. This lesson became clear on December 26, 2004, when a massive earthquake in the Indian Ocean touched off tsunami waves throughout South Asia.

To people on the beach in Phuket, Thailand, the first sign of anything unusual was when the tide suddenly receded, leaving 656 feet (200m) of exposed sand. It was as if a giant had sucked in just before exhaling. Within minutes, an enormous wall of water appeared in the distance, a wave like none of the tourists had ever seen. Its onslaught flattened huts and buildings, swept away cars, and engulfed those in its path. The giant wave was only the first of several to hit the coast that day. By evening, a long list of victims and the missing had been posted. Similar waves struck throughout the region. The total death toll from the giant waves exceeded a quarter million people.

THE TSUNAMI WARNING SYSTEM

Soon after the South Asia tsunamis, nations in the Indian Ocean region, including Japan, India, Indonesia, Thailand, and Sri Lanka, agreed to build an early warning system to detect huge waves while they are still many miles away from the coast. The planned system was based on the Tsunami Warning System in the Pacific basin.

Survivors salvage what they can from the rubble of the Indonesian city of Bandah Aceh, destroyed by the 2004 tsunami.

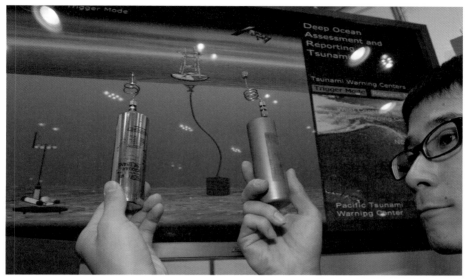

As part of the Tsunami Warning System, tsunameters like these are set on the seafloor to detect the slight changes in water pressure that occur when a tsunami passes overhead.

The Tsunami Warning System began as a response to a rash of deadly tsunamis in the Pacific basin in the 1960s. The system cost tens of millions of dollars to install and maintain, but has saved many lives. It is made up of a chain of pressure sensors on the ocean floor. Each sensor measures the weight of the water above it. Should a tsunami pass overhead, the tiny increase in pressure causes the sensor to signal a buoy on the ocean's surface. In turn, the buoy sends a signal to a satellite, which relays the alert to a manned center responsible for warning the public.

Eventually, the new Indian Ocean system may be even more effective than its predecessors elsewhere in the world. Scientists hope to link its sensors to sophisticated computer models and satellite monitors in order to forecast tsunamis minutes or even hours before they occur. Each extra minute could be invaluable in saving lives.

Scientists also realize that false alarms can occur. Three months after the Indian Ocean tsunamis, another massive earthquake struck

Tourists on a beach in Thailand sit next to a new tsunami warning system tower.

off the coast of Sumatra. This time, however, despite the 8.7 magnitude of the quake, no tsunami waves developed. Scientists were puzzled until they discovered that the second earthquake was deep-focus—that is, it took place in much deeper water, so it did not create the massive waves associated with tsunamis.

While advanced warning about potential tsunamis is important, another challenge is communicating the danger to people in harm's way. Sensors in the Pacific system actually picked up the earthquake in southern Asia as soon as it occurred. Calls were made to officials in several South Asian countries, including Thailand. The problem was getting the information to people rapidly—including fishermen and market vendors with no radios or telephones.

For all the effectiveness of sensors and satellites in detecting the earthquake, simpler technology might be a solution for this final step. Some communities are considering sirens or whistles to warn of an impending tsunami.

HURRICANES AND THE SAFFIR/SIMPSON SCALE

Like earthquakes and tsunamis, hurricanes can affect large numbers of people in a short time. A hurricane forms over very warm water (at least 80°F [26.6°C]) in the tropics. An area of low pressure is pushed northward by southern breezes called trade winds. At first, the storm may be no stronger than a thunderstorm, but if it crosses a long expanse of warm seawater for several days, it may intensify into a large area of low pressure called a tropical depression. Should the storm continue to expand, its clouds can grow to towering heights of 40,000 feet (12km). The low-pressure area can measure 400 miles (643km) or more across, spinning in a cyclonic movement around a 30-mile-long core (48km), or "eye." The storm has then become a hurricane. (In the western Pacific and Indian oceans, a hurricane is called a typhoon.)

THE NEXRAD SYSTEM

In the middle of the United States, in Norman, Oklahoma, lies the control center for one of the most powerful tools in predicting tornadoes and other dangerous storms. The resource is called Next Generation Weather Radar (NEXRAD). It is a nationwide system of Doppler radar stations.

The first installations of NEXRAD stations took place in the early 1990s. In 1996, the system was completed, and it now comprises 158 Doppler radar sites across the United States and at selected locations overseas. The sites are located at airports, weather stations, and military bases. Each site looks like a giant golf ball sitting atop a tower of scaffolding. It can generate remarkably clear, three-dimensional images of weather systems at a distance of 125 miles (201km), and, with some loss of resolution, of those up to 200 miles (322km) away. The NEXRAD sites have replaced the portable Doppler setups employed by storm chasers over the years.

NEXRAD instantly improved the reliability of storm predictions. Whereas previous radars had measured the shape and density of storms in a rough way, NEXRAD directly measures the rotating speed of air inside a cloud formation. With it, meteorologists can predict, with remarkable accuracy, the intensity and direction of tornadoes, allowing them to issue precise warnings much more quickly than ever before.

A crane installs a **NEXRAD** Doppler radar dome on a station in Utah.

Spinning counterclockwise around its eye, Hurricane Jeanne makes landfall over the state of Florida in 2004.

Forecasters use the Saffir/Simpson Hurricane Scale to measure the intensity of the storm. The scale goes from category 1 (winds of 74 to 95 miles per hour [119 to 153km/h]) to category 5 (winds of more than 155 miles per hour [249km/h]). Category 5 hurricanes do catastrophic damage to buildings and cause intense flooding.

Atlantic hurricanes and Asian typhoons occur most frequently between July and October, and they follow predictable paths. For example, in the Northern Hemisphere, hurricanes tend to form just above the equator and follow a route that leads from the Caribbean islands to the Gulf of Mexico or to Florida and up the eastern coast of the United States. The most destructive hurricane on record in the United States was Hurricane Andrew in 1992. The storm caused $26.5 billion in damage and left 26 people dead in the United States and the Bahamas.

TOOLS FOR HURRICANE PREDICTION

The ability of satellites in space to identify and track hurricanes like Andrew is a powerful forecasting tool. In the past, news of a tropical storm over the ocean depended on a sighting by ship or, more rarely, from an aircraft. Today, satellite images show the basic features of a tropical storm as soon as it forms. In fact, meteorologists look for telltale cloud developments that indicate a storm is possible. Cloud movements also reveal the strength and direction of tropical winds.

This radar image provides a detailed look at Hurricane Frances over Florida and the amount of rainfall associated with the storm.

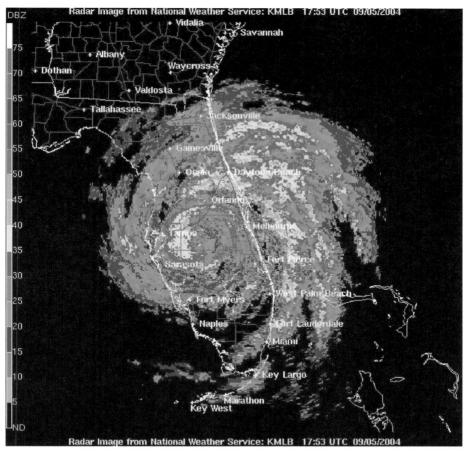

Radar Image from National Weather Service: KMLB 17:53 UTC 09/05/2004

Once a tropical depression has grown into a tropical storm and nears the North American continent, aircraft begin to monitor it. The U.S. Air Force Reserve employs hurricane-tracking planes that fly through the storm and measure wind speed and pressure. They also locate and measure the eye of the storm. Once radioed to an operations center in Miami, this information adds details about the storm's interior to the meteorologists' growing charts that describe the storm's progress.

Nearer to land, the storm enters the range of onshore radar. The radar emits electromagnetic waves, the same as light and radio waves. As the waves bounce off the storm and back to the receiver, they describe the storm's shape and its precise distance away.

Improved radar helps meteorologists map storms, and often predict their paths, with great accuracy. The Doppler radar system measures the frequency of reflected waves more precisely than ordinary radar. It can tell exactly how fast and in what direction a storm is moving. Doppler signals are translated into colors on computer screens—the more vivid the colors, the faster the storm is moving.

Doppler radar and satellite images are also important in forecasting tornadoes and other inland storms. In Tornado Alley, the midsection of the United States where tornadoes occur most frequently, Doppler radar has enabled meteorologists to issue tornado warnings minutes faster than ever before—precious minutes that allow people to seek shelter and remain safe.

CHAPTER 3

THE FUTURE OF PREDICTING NATURAL DISASTERS

Geologists and other scientists have many different ideas about the best approach to predicting earthquakes. Most agree on one thing, however: The ability to predict the exact date of an earthquake will not come anytime soon. Since the acceptance of the plate tectonics theory, researchers have struggled to understand the physics of earthquakes. They emphasize that earthquake prediction is not like weather forecasting. Earthquakes do not occur in particular seasons, and they do not seem to follow an identifiable pattern, the way storm systems move across a map. They strike suddenly, with no warning.

A scientist sets up a GPS station on Washington's Mount St. Helens to help measure seismic activity in the area.

Nevertheless, scientists continue to investigate different methods of predicting earthquakes more precisely. The most fruitful approach in the near future appears to be long-range forecasts, or hazard assessments, that identify areas where strikes are most likely. Nevertheless, some researchers are pursuing ideas that may one day enable scientists to predict earthquakes within days or hours.

THE GLOBAL EARTHQUAKE SATELLITE SYSTEM

One of the most promising technologies is a new satellite system, the Global Earthquake Satellite System (GESS), which includes a new kind of radar called InSAR. The radar would provide scientists with extremely detailed images of broad regions of the earth. Using InSAR, scientists could compare overlapping images of an area day after day. Using this method, they could detect slight changes in the land surface—as minimal as 2 inches (5cm). These changes, or deformations, might indicate built-up strain in the earth's crust that could lead to an earthquake.

The space shuttle has already employed InSAR to make detailed topographic maps of the earth's surface. In addition, NASA is considering a proposal to launch a new satellite equipped with InSAR. Geologists hope someday to have a constellation of InSAR-equipped satellites orbiting the earth. These could provide dense sets of data for every earthquake-prone area on the planet.

Scientists believe that InSAR and other satellite monitors might even be able to detect slow signs of stress relief along fault lines. They know that sliding plates along a fault line release energy suddenly in an earthquake. They now believe that stress is also relieved gradually in a slower process. InSAR might help scientists predict more dangerous build-ups of stress elsewhere in the fault system beneath the earth.

ELECTROMAGNETIC SIGNALS TO PREDICT EARTHQUAKES

A team of Greek scientists is taking a more controversial approach to earthquake prediction. Panayiotis Varotsos, Kessar Alexopoulos, and Konstantine Nomicos of Athens University think they can predict earthquakes by reading the electrical and magnetic activity in the ground. Their idea is that rocks, which have a measurable electric charge, develop tiny cracks when under seismic stress. The cracks widen and admit water as the stress increases, causing the rocks to expand. Thus, rocks under the stress of a potential

This InSAR radar image of California's San Andreas Fault was taken by the space shuttle. Such images may help scientists predict earthquakes.

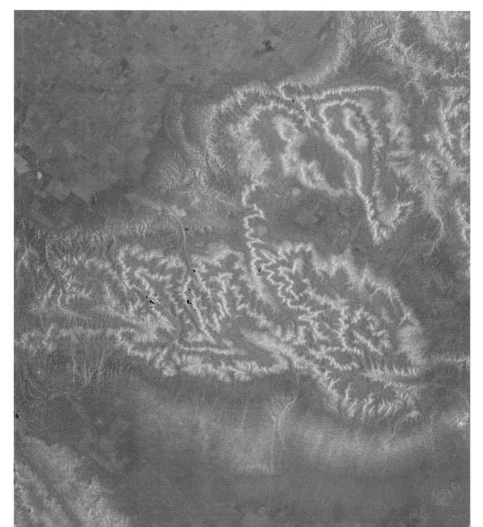

CAN ANIMALS PREDICT AN EARTHQUAKE?

Seismologists, using the most sophisticated equipment available, admit they are unable to predict when an earthquake is about to occur. Can cats and dogs do better?

Down through the centuries, there have been stories about animals anticipating quakes. Greek historians write that in 373 B.C. weasels, snakes, and rats fled the Greek city of Helice just before a powerful earthquake leveled it. In other accounts, chickens have stopped laying eggs and fish have thrashed in the water prior to tremors. Pet owners of today have reported seeing their dogs or cats whining or acting skittish just before an earthquake.

Some have theorized that animals sense slight tremors or foreshocks that humans cannot detect. In

Monitoring the behavior of geese and other animals may help geologists predict seismic activity.

Household pets such as cats and dogs seem to be able to sense tremors that people cannot perceive.

Japan, where earthquakes happen frequently, researchers have studied animal reactions closely in a quest to learn just what signs the creatures are responding to.

Most seismologists remain skeptical, however. Panicky behavior in animals, they say, could be caused by any number of things, including hunger and fear of predators. Furthermore, people tend to recall odd behavior that happens right before a major event like an earthquake—and forget that the same activity also happens on ordinary days.

Still, researchers in many countries are looking into the phenomenon. Perhaps a few supercomputers could one day be replaced by a caged bird or a high-strung housecat.

Greek scientists are investigating the possibility of measuring electromagnetic changes in the ground as a way of predicting earthquakes, like the one that destroyed this factory in Athens in 1999.

earthquake would emit different electrical and magnetic information than usual. The Greek scientists call these voltages seismic electric signals

Most earthquake researchers dismissed the Greeks' work as wishful thinking. However, a team from Japan's Earthquake Prediction Research Center made a startling discovery. In March 2000, using telephone wires as sensitive antennas, the team detected unusual changes in the electromagnetic fields in Japan's Izu Islands. The changes in the fields grew in intensity for two months, when a series of quakes struck the islands. After the seismic event, the signals returned to normal.

Even allowing for other causes, such as rainfall or man-made signals, the Japanese scientists could not explain the spike in electrical and magnetic fields. The Greek scientists insist that this is the same phenomenon they have been observing in their own country. Most scientists remain unconvinced, although some allow that it is a promising area for further research.

BROADBAND EARTHQUAKE MONITORS

The earth's oceans, which until recently represented a large gap in seismic information, provide another promising field for earthquake research. Tremors and earthquakes beneath the sea have been off-limits to curious scientists. A new technology, however, may soon fill that gap. Scientists at the University of California, Berkeley, have designed state-of-the-art broadband seismometers to be placed on the ocean floor. The sensors in the device can measure vibrations so faint that they last only a tenth of a second.

The new seismometers are so sensitive—and prone to interference from ocean currents and wind-generated waves and surf—that they have to be positioned very carefully. To do this, engineers employ a remote-controlled vehicle. On the ocean floor, the vehicle digs a 2-foot-deep (0.6m) hole, places a plastic pipe inside it, and lowers the seismometer into the pipe. The device is then covered with glass beads to stabilize it and protect it from ocean currents. A separate device to record data is placed 30 feet (9m) away so that its own vibrations do not affect the sensors.

Scientists lower a deep-sea seismometer into the ocean. Such monitors are designed to register even the faintest tremors.

EARTHQUAKE IN THE SKY

The challenges faced by forecasters of earthquakes and storms are opposites. While seismologists have success predicting long-range probabilities for earthquakes in an area, they are stumped in the short term. On the other hand, meteorologists do well with daily and weekly forecasts, but flunk when they attempt climate models for future years.

Now Kim Christensen and two other London physicists are looking at probabilities associated with

Thunderstorms, like earthquakes, are caused by a buildup of energy that is released all at once with violent force.

Meteorologists are hopeful that long-range weather forecasting can be done using the same methods seismologists currently use to predict earthquakes.

earthquakes to improve long-range weather forecasting. The frequency of earthquakes is governed by a "power law." In other words, a quake ten times stronger than another should occur one-tenth as often. The scientists found that the same power law holds true for weather events such as rainfall.

Earthquakes and thunderstorms share one physical characteristic: They are both created by energy that builds to a certain threshold and then is released. Earthquake scientists use this idea to predict the likely number and intensity of earthquakes in an area over a long period of time. Christensen and his colleagues think the same forecasting could be done regarding major hurricanes, floods, and droughts. These long-range models could help communities at risk prepare for disasters.

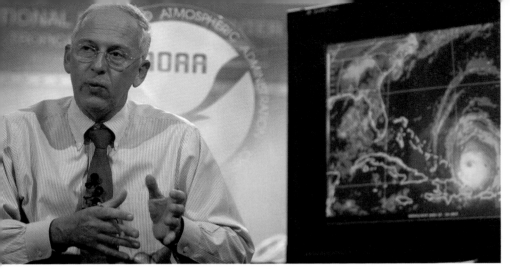

Meteorologists are using new technologies to improve their ability to forecast hurricanes.

Scientists hope one day to install a series of these devices around the globe. They could provide three-dimensional pictures of the earth's interior. They would also help forecast earthquakes and tsunamis that originate at midocean ridges.

CAMEX-4 AND THE INSIDE OF A HURRICANE

While seismologists are busy on the ocean floor, meteorologists are looking to space for improved storm prediction. NASA's Convection and Moisture Experiment (CAMEX-4) seeks to measure a hurricane in a new way. In 2001, as Hurricane Humberto roared over the Atlantic Ocean, NASA scientists fitted a high-altitude ER-2 aircraft with a special Doppler radar. The radar could read the shifting rain and ice particles inside a hurricane in order to measure its direction, air speed, and rain intensity. The ER-2 flew so high that the pilot had to wear a spacesuit. The result was the most accurate measurements of a hurricane ever, and a better knowledge of how such storms form and move.

In a separate experiment, an ER-2 pilot dropped sensors that looked like potato chip cans into a raging hurricane. The sensors measured the temperature at each level of the storm. This data helped scientists understand how heat from the condensation in clouds causes the air to expand and rise, fueling the formation of a hurricane. The temperature readings and ice particle data were combined to create computer simulations of a hurricane. By studying the computer models, scientists may be better able to predict future storms.

QUIKSCAT AND THE HURRICANE HUNTERS

Meteorologists strive to keep outdoing themselves in accurately tracking storms. The error rate is the difference between where a hurricane is predicted to strike 48 hours before it hits land and where it actually makes landfall. In 2004, forecasters at the National Hurricane Center hoped to improve their error rate by 10 miles (16km), which over the last ten years has averaged 139 miles (224km) from landfall. In reality, the forecasters cut that rate in half due to advances in numerical weather prediction and to the use of sophisticated computer models.

To keep the error rate going down, forecasters are looking at a range of new tools. NASA's $98 million Quick Scatterometer, or QuikSCAT, satellite can continually gauge ocean winds to monitor the speed and intensity of a hurricane more accurately. The QuikSCAT can also snap a detailed photo of a hurricane every six minutes. Forecasters receive additional data from human sources like the Hurricane Hunters, a group of air force reservists based in Biloxi, Mississippi. These intrepid pilots fly around-the-clock missions into the eyes of hurricanes over the Atlantic, gathering precious data from the center of the storms.

LIVING WITH NATURAL DISASTERS

Few events unite the people of the world like natural disasters. After the tsunamis that devastated South Asia in 2004, contributions for relief aid poured into agencies worldwide. Hurricanes that strike in the Caribbean and along the East Coast of the United States regularly elicit charitable aid for those caught in the storms' paths. People in the Midwest of the United States learn about tornado safety in grade school, while those on the West Coast live with the possibility that a devastating earthquake could strike at any time.

This radar image of a typhoon in the South Pacific shows wind speed and was taken by NASA's QuikSCAT satellite in 2004.

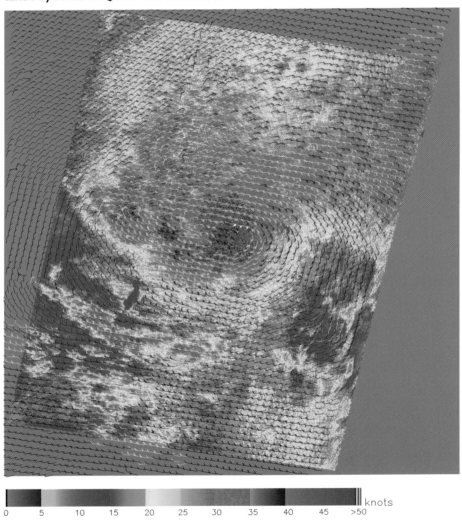

| 0 | 5 | 10 | 15 | 20 | 25 | 30 | 35 | 40 | 45 | >50 |
knots

A Thai official and an American aid worker prepare to install a tsunami warning siren on Phuket, an island off Thailand that was devastated by the 2004 tsunami.

Although scientists know a great deal about how disasters such as hurricanes, tsunamis, and earthquakes occur, much remains to be learned. New technologies, from satellites to improved radar to networks of supercomputers, reveal more about these events every year. Scientists can inform people about the probabilities of a deadly hurricane or earthquake in a given area. Nevertheless, predicting natural disasters with total accuracy remains a dream for the future. In the meantime, communities will use communications and warning systems to keep people safe when these destructive events occur.

GLOSSARY

Camex-4: NASA's Convection and Moisture Experiment, which reads the shifting rain and ice particles inside a hurricane.

Doppler radar: A radar system used to measure the speed and intensity of violent storms.

front: A mass of air.

InSAR: Radar that provides extremely detailed images of broad regions of the earth's surface.

mantle: A thick layer of rock and molten material that surrounds the hot core of the earth.

meteorology: The study of weather.

QuakeSim: A NASA program that uses computer models and satellite information to predict earthquakes.

Quick-Scat: Quick Scatterometer satellite, used to continually gauge ocean winds and photograph hurricanes.

radiosondes: Lightweight transmitters tethered to balloons and lifted into the atmosphere to send back data on temperature, air pressure, and humidity.

Richter scale: A mathematical scale for measuring the intensity of earthquakes, invented by an American named Charles Richter in 1935.

Rossby waves: Horizontal waves that follow the eastward movement of the air, like ocean tides.

Saffir/Simpson Hurricane Scale: A scale that measures the intensity of a hurricane.

seismology: The study of earthquakes.

seismometer: A device used to detect an earthquake, invented by the Italian Luigi Palmieri in 1855.

tectonic plates: Slabs inside the earth that float atop the mantle on molten material and slide past each other at different speeds

tsunami: A gigantic wave or series of waves produced by an earthquake in the middle of the ocean.

Tsunami Warning System: A system made up of a chain of pressure sensors on the ocean floor and buoys on the surface.

FOR FURTHER INFORMATION

Books

Mark Maslin, *Restless Planet: Earthquakes*. Austin: Raintree Steck-Vaughn, 2000. An introduction to earthquakes, their causes, and methods of predicting them.

D.M. Souza, *Powerful Waves*. Minneapolis: Carolrhoda Books, 1992. An overview of tsunamis, including how they form and what precautions can be taken against them.

Susan and Steven Wills, *Meteorology: Predicting the Weather*. Minneapolis: Oliver Press, 2004. A look at the pioneers of weather prediction, from Benjamin Franklin to today's storm chasers.

Web Sites

Hurricanes (www.fema.gov/kids/hurr.htm). A good general site about hurricanes, including how to rate their intensity, how they are tracked, and information about the largest hurricanes of the last century.

Understanding Earthquakes (www.crustal.ucsb.edu/ics/understanding). A collection of features about earthquakes, including the history of earthquakes, an animated globe with quake locations, and accounts of famous earthquakes.

INDEX

Alexopoulos, Kessar, 35, 38
animals, 36–37
Aristotle, 6

Bjerknes, Vilhelm, 17

Chang Heng, 6–7
Christensen, Kim, 40–41
communications, 17, 19
continental drift theory, 8–9
Convection and Moisture Experiment (CAMEX-4), 42

de Melo, Sebastião, 10–11
disasters
    explanations for, 6
    types of, 4
Doppler radar system, 28, 32, 42

dragon jars, 6–7

earthquakes
    cause of, 6
    frequency of, 41
    measuring, 39, 42
    predicting, 20–23, 33–38
    studying, 6–7, 10–15

fault lines, 14–15

Global Earthquake Satellite System (GESS), 34
Greeks, ancient, 6, 15, 36

hazard assessments, 21–22, 34
Howard, Luke, 16
hurricanes, 27, 30–32, 42–43

InSAR, 34
meteorology, 15
Milne, John, 13–14

Next Generation Weather Radar
    (NEXRAD), 28
Nomicos, Konstantine, 35, 38

Palmieri, Luigi, 11, 13–14
plate tectonics, 6, 8–9

QuakeSim, 22–23
Quick Scatterometer (QuikSCAT),
    43

radar systems, 28, 32, 34, 42
Richter, Charles, 12
Rossby, Carl-Gustaf, 17, 19

Saffir/Simpson Hurricane Scale, 30
seismoscopes/ seismographs/
    seismometers, 11, 13–14, 39, 42

toll of disasters, 4–5, 7, 10
tornadoes, 28, 32
tropical depressions, 27, 32
tsunamis, 10, 12
Tsunami Warning System, 23, 25, 27

U.S. Geological Survey, 21–22

Varotsos, Panayiotis, 35, 38

weather predictions, 15–17, 19, 28, 41,
    43
Wegener, Alfred, 8–9
World-Wide Standard Seismological
    Network, 14

ABOUT THE AUTHOR

John Allen is a writer who lives in Oklahoma City. His other books for Blackbirch Press include *Idi Amin* and *High-Tech Weapons*.